FOUR CITIES

Garrett,

Thanks for the
support!
Hope you enjoy!

xoxo

FOUR CITIES

HALA ALYAN

Black
Lawrence
Press

Black Lawrence Press

www.blacklawrence.com

Executive Editor: Diane Goettel
Book and cover design: Amy Freels
Cover art: Zeina Koreitem.

Copyright © 2015 Hala Alyan
ISBN: 978-1-62557-939-3

Published 2015 by Black Lawrence Press.
Printed in the United States.

Grateful acknowledgment is made to the editors of the journals below, where the following poems appear or are forthcoming, sometimes in different forms.
CALYX Journal: "Al Aqsa"
Copper Nickel: "Junebug"
Matter: "A Dream in Seville," "Winter Altar"
Mizna: "Meimei," "Souvenirs"
Painted Bride Quarterly: "Apology," "Aubade," "Of the MRI Images for My Abdomen"
Plume: "After Thunderstorms in Oklahoma"
Poetry Bay: "Happy"
Shahadat: "One Conversation in April," "For Flinching"
Southword Journal: "Dinner"
The Guidebook: "On My Shoulder a Bruise Yellows," "In the Ocean, Our Legs are Green"
The Literary Bohemian: "Marketplace"
The Understanding between Foxes and Light (Anthology): "Push"
Third Coast: "Not Snow, Not Sun"
Tongue: A Journal of Writing & Art: "Forgive Your Gods"

For Johnny,
who changed everything

Contents

Music

The Japanese woman plays with a beatific smile,
spotlight bluish on the stage. In between songs
she tells us about her father, who once found a black cat
and named him *Sparrow*. The violin dips and rises
in her hands. Tiny hands. Like creatures skittering up
and down the long sweeping neck. Across the table,
a man touches my fingers, but I pull them back,
rebraid my hair. The waitress brings us clams, open-
chested, brothed in lemon. I eat with urgency.
The bread is good. During the intermission, the man
asks about the music and I am uncharacteristically honest.
It makes me sad. The man is confused. *Like rain,* I offer.
In Beirut, when the gunfire began, we blared hip-hop
music and dragged furniture away from the window.
We poured vodka in iceless glasses. One girl drew with red
ink a circus tree while the rest of us huddled on the balcony,
mimicking the soft *oh* of a Georgian accent. I sponge
lemon with the crust of bread and wait for the slow
music to begin once more. I want to love this man,
his hands and his questions, to explain the malaise of
Mediterranean rainfall, but I made promises once and yes,
darling, yes, damnit, I remember: our mouths shy
beneath the display of bombwork, the muffled light of
fishing boats, the debris, the cats—always—mewling.

I

Encounters

The snapdragons bloomed that night.

Every year, the people cluster around the skating rink,
the tree, the carnival lights.
I think you met me on a ferryboat in Paris,
one hundred years ago.

We are the island in the distance.

A storm forks the city into three. Beirut never
saved me. Balconies overlooking
sea, every sky a brittle eye, here where the muezzin
sings only for the dead.

I wore yellow. You saw me and thought of gardens.

Weather

Lately, I've been dreaming of
an elfish girl diving for lungs.

She is my granddaughter.
In the dream I am always cold and

she comes to me with purple hands.
I exclaim, fret, upend a basket for soap,

but only find chalk. She laughs.
You said to bring you something radiant.

Birthday Art

Not jungle, but pastel, the color
of the first bruise paled
beneath the second. Mama,
I want to be a woman of dusklit
mosques, of ginger prickly in tea,
steam netted for a lover. Sky
becomes circular, spans itself
like hair. Hair, thickets, copper
with pollen: the mouth is a
key in the shape of echo. Rouge,
coral, center the suns. He
terraces bones for invisible
gods, blackening with
shale. And then a stream,
chromophilous water. Rinsing
the form, nipples dark as
coins hidden in a silk purse.
The backcloth is spent, another
flimsy dream about a doll
factory in Beirut, sirens lighting
the empty birdcage. My dream
self tastes the Turkish coffee:
graphite. Some treetop
ornaments with paper cranes
dangling from wires until wind
rustles all that white into a
froth like steam or cresting wave.
Like something spilled.
On a bed. Where bodies dance.

All morning, the fight:

my eyes elsewhere, and the god you invoked.
The souk will burn tomorrow. Where did we bury
the moth? I am meant to keep quiet about the lemongrass,
growing godless and wild from even the slimmest cracks of sidewalk.
In December, the museum is garnished as a bride.
Something awful has happened here: a lost electricity.
Two men wander my street. The collapse was three years ago.
My belts hung loose around hipbone. Our faces lanterned.
We never grasped that city, even as we sat in her toes,
kissing. The men do not write. I am to them a toxin,
a liar with the canvassed truth. I touch the sassafras and cry.

Sisyphus on the Letterhead

In ghosthood we sparkplug car radios,
startle the living with static

and bluegrass music. With banshee hair
I found you testing the microphone,

roping cable wires as rain glazed
the Village into an ornament.

God lives in the marshland.
The Mediterranean slides her ugly,

green tongue towards the city and you
sleep against the window

of an airplane. What is your decoy,
your empty thing? Cutting a deck of cards,

or waking pyretic to dawn. Equator
beneath a patch of horses. Fate,

that handsome word, was us eating
baklava. Magician's secret:

beneath mirrors are hideaways. Always.

Push

Gaza. I'm sorry.   *Beirut.* I still love you like an arsonist
Venice. When that glassblower put his lips to the glowing pipe and I
followed his breath into an ornament I understood grace.
New Orleans. Faintly biblical. Swelter and melody and staircase.
Boston. I found the bird already dead crooked nest scattering the
pavement and for days all I saw was that constellation of bones.
Aya Nappa. I cannot hear your name without thinking war and ship
and two moons before coastline. *Tripoli.* It was whiplash.
Rome. When I think of my future self she is walking your piazza
wearing something yellow.   *Wichita.* The car rides
through your highway backbone. Always a thunderstorm.
Gaza. I'm sorry.   *Ramallah.* Thank you for the applause.
Seltzer water and tableh player. Tomato and bread. Thank you for the
balcony.   *Dubai.* I forgot a scarf a silver ring a tube of lipstick.
The rest you may keep.   *Aleppo.* Forgive me my litter. My uneaten
rice. My abundance of light bulbs.   *Baghdad.* Twenty
six years and you still make me cry.   *Doha.*
Starlit eels and honey water. I miss those colors.   *Istanbul.*
Marry me.   *Dallas.* I pretended I was Aladdin turning
the soil over and gasping.   *Gaza.* I'm sorry. *Beirut.* You are
cherry end of cigarette. Push and tunnel. How can you fit so much?
          Norman, Oklahoma. No one calls me Holly anymore.
          Brooklyn. Sixty-two books and mistakes. You showed me
where to sit.   *Dublin.* Someday.   *Damas-*
cus. Nothing is as dangerous as an unlit match. You taught us that.
Paris. By beauty I meant that bridge. My brother's legs over the
water.   *Jerusalem.* Only you know what I am capable of.
London. I wasn't ungrateful.   *Gaza.* I'm sorry.   *Manhat-*

tan. Myself in that nightclub. A paper crane with a beating heart. Do not wake her.   *Bangkok*. I ate your fruit salted. Shrines of gold and sugar.   *Beirut*. I bruise as easily as you do. We are both anemic veins and unbrushed hair.   *Gaza*. I'll tell you where I've been.

Let Me Put It This Way

A woman sits
with black draped
across her shoulders
and an eastern moon
blinking white above her.
All day she sifted
through rubble for the gleam
of her mother's silver, knife
or ladle to rinse in the river.
Her child lies beneath soil,
sharing rain with tree
roots. A woman sits
with black draped across her
shoulders. She lights a cigarette
and exhales a feather of smoke.
          Says, God,
God is greater.

Ballad for Kissing Beneath the Tawdry Fireworks

Storm's coming
and I am the insect siphoning sugar from plant.

In Doha it never rained. The teacups filled with steam.

Gemmayze glistens with water and streaks
of pink light.

Our six little ghosts usher around us. Yours,
with the ample hips of the well-fed. Mine crowd a stranger's lighter.

Dazzling yolks make acoustic suns. In your dream I potted

poisonous shrubs in a circle.
The purple berries I pressed onto white bread.

This confetti sky reminds us both of February and liquid
in the gaps of our spines.

I lipstick for our dinner.
I gather my hair up plump as a raindrop.

Against your neon body I scatter lips hands breath.
I am the fable with a mouth.

Winter Altar

The last Sunday of the month pockets
of roses

appear on the lamppost.

I line windowsills with ash

because I cannot bear the
carcasses.

They torched the library in
Baghdad

and I am proud of the tea I swirled
with milk

the night you left. Soap

soaps a sink of plants flecking
the clay basin and

faltered. I script every stalled train
into romance.

I do ballerina stretches.

I twirl
for every smiling man.

They will all die. I know that now.

You, Bonsai Girl

Blue was always
yours,

jazzing its way onto your buttons
and eyelids.

Some women dream of hurricane.

I think you are a pier,
filmed, wooden planks beneath sheets of rain.

Or some jungle canopy,

wolfing light while, below,
creatures twist in the murk. Anyway,

what remains of that hunting is inland.

Some gourd,
emptied, your September ancestors

howling on Delancey. Stale Nile water in your mouth,

dark as sunflowers. (The heart, not the petal.)
I hear you, ghost,

your voice minnowing the sag of mattress

even in America. Prophecy,
how you held your body still in his bed

like you were no woman, but object.
A tooth,

long and
yellow, pulled from a witch's

garden and oh
sister it was real. That sky. Those streets full of men

applauding your legs.

Icon

While the moon stoops in the early April sky,
I fold paper into a tragic crane. One magician
burns sand, another palms a tree. My crane
flickers her lovely neck and weeps. After the fire,
everything smelled of brick, a red that
guttered in the neighbor's dreams. A piano
turns bodies magnetic with music. I want to break
myself like egg for you, to pool in gold and lost.

Sestina for December

Miles to the east there is a carnival of green—
whistling men drink *arak* and toast to God.
I trace for you another weather, a coastline framed with salt
and some garland of clouds. Gossamer, wispy as cake.
But here it is always nightfall, sirens staining the air
and that ugly moment of ice, against glass, against mouth.

A wrecking ball, you, with that arctic mouth
and limber legs. Beneath the white you are green-
breasted as a planet whispering with air.
Ashen stars reveal the bridge and the subway flyer says *God
Loves You.* Loves the cinders, the snowflakes cake
my balcony in Brooklyn. I see the white and think salt.

The orange-jacketed men wake at dawn and pour salt
out of trucks onto the roads, fog from their mouths
as they curse and wait for melting. Ocean is cake
batter in moonlight: lathered, flecks of green
like a dusting of eelgrass. God
knows better, scatters insect wings in the air

and falling to my boots. I hate this air,
graphite chamber with no daylight. Some salt-
lick for a dumb creature, ecstasy murmuring God's
name against the red seeds. We chapel with our mouths.
Where are the small miracles? Praise the storm sky green,
the heel of good bread inside the cardboard cake.

In the supermarket, I buy the makings of a cake:
frosting, milk, sugar to thaw the kitchen air.
I will eat alone, bite after bite, a mug of green
tea after. For one afternoon, I will give my plate no salt.
Vanilla, the dough is lattice in my mouth
while the oven blinks and glows like a little god.

My mother mails me envelopes across the ocean: God
necklaces, gold pendants, calligraphy intricate as wedding cake.
I wear the lovely blue eye, the verse about a mouth.
But even the holy jewelry becomes ice: such air
turns any earring into a hammer. I write my mother about you, salt
my tongue along the envelope glue. The ink is mermaid green

and even as I write *cake* I am remembering the air
of July, the tiny gods that waded with me in Haifa's sea. Salt:
I did not close my mouth. I ate every crumb of green.

Narcissus

The clouds owl-eye the sky,
gaped at by moon. Yes,

I dreamt we wed. A priest
fed us rice and sugar,

the cathedral was locked.
Trees litter Brooklyn streets

with blossoms. I wake to Iraq,
to neighbors kissing.

I am a ghost ship
smothered by Neruda's stars.

Is that what you wanted?
To hear me say I ache? I ache.

Not Snow, Not Sun

Sea glass flits through the sand like the halo
of grenades, glistening with ordinary colors. A rocket

falls in Tel Aviv, a bearded man lifts his arm, a village
near Saida eats ash for a week. And your smile—

it split open like a sky that March, the first
of the decade. Your hand swam over my knee, forearm,

neck. Even the plundered would have smiled
at our singing, the trees flush above our heads like a

parasol. We must have looked careless, licking jam
from our fingers, tallying what we could not forgive.

I kept a bullet from that spring and bought some velvet
for a necklace, the metal chandeliering between

my breasts. But the steel rusted and I keep it in
a cactus pot now. Let it sprout: Some metal-

lipped flower, land sprung forth, or a single bulb,
hairless and green, or flame, flame the size of lungs.

From My Grandmother's Balcony, *Beyada*

The lance of a car honk slices the air
angrily and a dark head emerges from the
window of a silver car. *Your mother's vagina,*
the man pitches Arabic expletives into the dusk
swiftly. Another man hurls from the corner store
with a thick steel pipe in his fist. He lifts it, shakes.
From up here, I am of no use to anyone. The
ambulance would take hours, there is no police
station. The men eye one another, snarling curses.
I clasp the balcony railing. A third man, laughing,
walks from the store, hands each man a cigarette,
says something quick and soft. Like clockwork,
the trio of heads swivel up, to the balcony, to me
watching. At a loss, I grin, wave. The men laugh,
raise their hands in return. One, teasing, signals
with his hand for me to come down. I shake my
head. *Impossible,* I motion. *But be safe. Go.* I wish
there was a gesture for *Don't curse at men
who carry metal. Your mothers love you.* But I keep
smiling, walk away from the railing, out of sight.
The sun is dim now, coffee candy, ugly copper.
Telephone wires and poles and antennas
block the view. Are the view.

Apology

They are burning tires in Tripoli.
    I bought new perfume, sulfurous,

the bottle of clouded glass. Know this:
    yours is the name that slid first to my lips

when the light became enormous
    and the anxious voices flared

like starlings, dozens of them, alit,
    alit. Only the rubber melts. Steel only chars

and the eclipse was disappointing,
    just moon rags and that vague smell of lemon.

After

Such snow in April.
We stand like citrus trees
with sugar in our bellies.
Each branch is wire.
How a greedy thing unfolds
her tongue cool as a spoon
until the bread moistens.
Soft enough to chew
the ice sags wilting
like wet bamboo. It would
be enough to be hunted
and kept with white amulets
in the plush of a basket,
they ruthless of me a stone
for other women, weary,
tired from the tracking.

And in Iraq, Fires

In another city, we would call this *flood*.
Instead it is just *rain*, housefuls of it
making pockets of the shore. The waves fume.
Some feverish belly,
a lit mouth through the window.
Bridge, umbrella, a better November.
We want crisis. Childhood without the sugar castle,
the forest of birds. Seven nationalities yoked
together in this cavern,
we are frantic with love.
I am the slack one, eating a plum without washing
it and writing a song for Hagar waiting
with bare mouth to kiss the ankle
of soil. Every war is a fête
and the thunder parrots itself.
Below find rivers dappled with trash, white
and blue, find the water
puckering in sewers that tumbles,
licks our sneakers. Parchment family,
we meet where the wood darkens, ash
powdering our fingertips like kohl.
Always, a television flickers. Theater beneath the glass,
it is kaleidoscope. It is kaleidoscope.
They die, they are always dying,
pleating tin to scrape bone from pavement.
In the garden beneath timber, I brush my hair.
The American boys practice their Arabic.

One Conversation in May

Tea, courtyard
in Hamra. A long row

of trees quirk their
shoulders to the sky and

she tells me I must taste mint
in Palestine. Yesterday, a storm,

and the roads are still littered
with branches and the

papered faces of Hezbollah
martyrs. She has a mouth

the Victorians would call
tragic, downturned and full.

She flinches. *And God?*
Does He want this?

She means the
protests. She means the men

with matches.
O to be a beachcomber,

plucking dazed the
starfish from her gritty palace.

I ask for salt before I
taste the rice.

*Would you rather be his muse
or his wife*? she asks.

Rain again, clouds blanching.
A single white hair,

glossy—my grandmother's
cat—clings to my

sweater. I flick at it. *Muse,*
but I am lying.

A Dream in Seville

It was as gilded as fishskin—

us, sea rising in tulip waves.
A minaret cloaked in fog.

Our voices lunar as we cry
each other's names, rapture

and protest,
our bodies gates in a cave.

I am barefoot amongst poppies.
Each star is a dagger, shards

from an urn broken
by a drunken god.

Forgive Your Gods

i.
Temple was the jade figurine
        around my neck lightly held by
thread the color
           of lobster heart.

Worried like *misbaha*, the same love-
prayer
        against the pad of my thumb. *Oh please let. Oh won't.*
Beirut from the balcony lies
        spangled as some sugared fruit.

That citrus smell mantling my bed for days.

ii.
Requiem Aeternam dona eis for the men the ocean ate,
swaying on dark ships from the Levant
        to Rome.
                Allah is pastoral in my hand, soft as flannel,
as the curl of grass across water.
        There are fires set in Gaza. Rage is the soup

that keeps some alive.

iii.
My aunt arrives tipsy and rapturous,
        speaking of love in my grandmother's kitchen.

We light cigarettes, spoon black olives from the jar.
      She pours an inch of whiskey,
shows me her new earrings, a gift. I am wary:

                Silver turns green in sun.

That night, I lie watching
dawn beneath the curtains, flinching
      from the twinge in my abdomen as muscles stitch

and I bleed.

iv.
      Sunbirds leave feathers outside the bar's entrance
and I find one on my boot.
Someone has been here with pen,
      emblazoned
        Forgive your gods

on the bar bathroom stall.

v.
Reem—
      Athena was cruel,
she kept men waiting with love elephantine.
Me,

I'm a Persephone girl,
        all theater and staircase and sulky luck,
running through rain to arrive at his doorway

with sodden slippers
saying

The movie was awful and I'm scared.

Ya Bint

It was Lyra peeking through the trees
in Berlin, a smattering of needlepoint lights
above the spiked leaves. You spoke of Io, steam-
plumes grainy as past. Of the past, keep the echo,
the blankness on a crested sand dune. I never
called you beautiful, though you are, starlet
lips and curls like earth, as though Baghdad
never forgot you. In the bowels of Gaza my father
counted chicks on a road. I am always pirating
his memories. You pointed to the brightest dot,
silver upon your wrist. Before your mother died,
she would extract fish bones, one after the
other, giving you the good, clean meat. I do not
remember the name of that star or the trees or
the man who bought us gin in a dank Irish
pub. The star was clear. I still think of your lips
and those glistening bones. All that almost-malice.

Z, at a Diner in Michigan

He likes the Greeks:
>   Heraclitus tailing the river and did I know
>   the leaves were not leaves

but birds?

Sixty-two years old and he carried all of Jenin
on his back
>   stacking

boxes and wire in the desolate backyard
of a Detroit split-level.

On the fourth of July
he unpops the tab of Coors cans

and gathers his daughters—he calls them *little
dears*—to watch the
>   colors

spearing over the lake.
>   He shows me where he sewed a flag

on the sleeve of his jacket. For when the drunk frat boys
lurch into his diner hissing

terrorist.

Even in blizzards he plods to the mosque past the mall
and picks up donuts on the way
        home.

Yes, the rain still reminds him of copper
pot boiling water for tea

        in his mother's kitchen and yes
the white of crumbling towers and lit

Iraqi skyline gritted his throat but
        see
see how divine the laughter trails from children

flurrying down hills of snow
in their puffy coats?

I let him pile my plate with tomatoes and
eggplant
        and *mjadara*. I want to tell him I wrote a name

not a wish
on that scrap of paper

        I hid between the stones. I want to say teach

me how to love one country
without hating the other.

Portrait of Love as a Series of Dreamscapes

i.
A mermaid shakes coins loose from her hair like sand.
She dives straight

into the ocean's throat.
I taste envy like saffron.

In my hands the coins become spiders.

ii.
There are butterfly trees in cities now,
flurried bodies

strung from branch tips.

Mammoth oaks shimmy
with the bristling of wings.

No one sweeps the carcasses when they fall.

iii.
The fire is cold, and has a voice.
San Francisco becomes Berlin becomes Dubai.

From a wooden tower we watch the dunes.

Habibi, the fire says. Or I.

iv.
A waitress brings a plate of reed leaves and eggs.

The carpet is mottled with crane light.
An orchid grows inside me.

I hold the wailing flower to my breast.

v.
A cat spooks a centipede into all directions.
I count ten million legs.

Outside the window clouds spin snow
an amphetamine white.

He's glossed as Halloween.

He kisses my neck
and a moon glares at us from the lake.

vi.
I remember the mermaid.

I am a prince and I charge the aquarium
calling her name.

Bubbles float from fish as red as apples.

A girl sits near the jellyfish tank surrounded
by tarot cards.

She is the mermaid a hundred years ago.

She taps a card and I turn it.
Sickle.

vii.
Asters skirt a line of trash cans.

It is dawn, somewhere on Jupiter.
The petals open and close like gills.

When insects mouth the nectar
there is a sound like mammals breeding.

Meimei

I.

In my grandmother's dream,
her father perches kind and
smiling on her bed.
He tells her not to worry, my daughter,
my daughter, you are safe,
don't be scared.

II.

For weeks after the accident
a man hurtled around my
grandmother's room. He was spectral,
she says, crawling on the walls
and the ceilings. When she screamed
it came out like bird wings beating
Even at noon she cannot bear the sound
of bare feet walking the marble floors.

III.

The same Turkish soap opera
is on the television set
in the living room and the one in the
bar and the one in the
Syrian bakery. The same
grey-eyed woman weeps as
she throws a glass and the same child
is still lost.

IV.

A girl needs to marry, she says.
Not love, you understand, but
for family, for when maps fold and
countries vanish and it is just you
and the dust you carry on your skin.
She touches the sun in my hair. Hala,
she says, if being a wife is dew and
life is the tin of cup and kettle,
then you need to dip your head,
you need to drink.

V.

She says, I knew a woman who
moved to India for a man, for love. Of
course, cries the Palestinian nurse who
rubs my grandmother's hands and spars
with the bathtub faucet until the water
is warm and strong. The nurse exhales
smoke skyward on the balcony and
looks directly at me. Do women ever
do anything for another reason?

VI.

When my grandmother fell and
cracked her skull on the sink,
she pulled at the floor with her arms even
as her sight faded and the pain hummed
her veins. The maid screamed when she
saw the red, everywhere. Life and death,
my grandmother says, run alongside
one another. Death is not dark or wicked,

it is good. Still, she says, still, when I fell
and blood filled my mouth, I was so
scared. I wanted to live.

VII.
Before my mother, there was
another daughter. Jaffa.
So tiny, my grandmother says, lived
for only thirty-three days. That was in
the desert, she says, before it crumbled
apart, before they lost that home, and
the one after that, and the one
after that.

VIII.
Anyways, she says,
it was the *ajanib* that drew Jordan. Syria.
She sighs. They gave us costumes
and we wore them.

IX.
Hala, when will you finish
your degree? And you walk at night
alone, even with those buildings large
as teeth? You're coming back
when you finish, I know you are. What
could you want that is not in this country,
in this sea and this mountain? May Allah give
you every mercy, every blessing. Don't
fall in love with America, okay? Good
girl, you are a good girl.

In the Ocean, Our Arms are Green

Lettered in the spine of a cookbook,
I am coy with secret:

It was always the
tiger
         behind the door.

Up north are the tiny
lakes, thickly wooded and petted

by God.

There are dandelion seeds parachuting
through the air.
            Flesh ill in dawn light, Monet

begged for more canvas to capture—
finally—
            the blue.

I'd like to vanish, too.
Earth scalping
            its fingernails,

that scratching sound
of grace. Atalanta surfaced

from the forest with barbed pelt
dangling
        and I am still coiled in the
        scuff marks

of your bathtub,
soap-ringed.

Perhaps a false ghost. I kiss you in the freezer.

I am the bread you are
        dipping now.

I am the oil.

Aubade

Dancing until the sky darted with gold, eardrums pulse
echoes. Even the *muezzin* is muted, underwater humming
as men carry fires for prickly pears and drum each engine
into a snare bass. Up ahead the buildings spire into their ugly
gray, drops of water startle from the cloudless sky—
laundry dribbling from clothespins, or condensation from
whirring air conditioners, jutting like jaws outside
the windows. A shopkeeper calls out *manousheh manousheh*
and the bread appears like trickery, steaming between teeth.
Already the casino seems distant, a faint vision of music snaking
the frantic sweating bodies. No viola skittering the parking lot,
just the streets whiffed with jasmine and diesel, just the creaking
of chains wound and lifted for window displays of lamb flank,
turquoise necklace, an armless mannequin. Just the road
turning, softly, the mound of earth that gives and slopes
to the clearing of red flowers, the gnats and oh the water.

Junebug,

or something else that glows.
A miniature seahorse,
incandescent tail twitching in
a snow globe, or some ocean
matron: firefly squid,
tentacles palpitating wildly,
sloshing water
salted with limestone
in your bathtub. Love,
I hunt a Valentine that will flare.
Like your daughter's name. *Boise*:
in French, it means wooded.
Or the gingko in October.
Each blazing leaf,
a shock of yellow shedding
confetti on the soil.
If I were braver—a Scorpio woman
or sailor—I would go to Hawaii
with a bucket and glass comb,
searching cream sand for the yards of
seaweed, luminous with tiny
burning bodies.
And then a needle and a steady hand,
until the crimson
seaweed stitches my braids, ropes
my flesh like a gown, until I stand
on your lawn naked as tundra
waiting for the sun to rise
on me, lit like a moon.

Summer

—violet hems the terrace,
a piazza of song, count
wasps in the summer, jasper misting
into something soft. At nightfall
the primrose coils and opens,
dragonflies jouncing into the stone
that encircles us. Wings against pebble,
clattering to their lover's bed
like a toy. Not a single fruit falls easily
into our palms from the bramble
awning. We have to touch the bark.
We shake and shake—

Dinner

Like lions we circle. A sundew plant dangles.
Green neck with long curling filaments

unfurling like steam in a chemist's test tube.
I want the slow awakening, that life of marveling,

to follow a man down a dark hallway, watch him dip
his face, his neck, into the water, flicking it over his

wrists. I want god, I want God, to bury myself
towards the swarming. Tomatoes

or cucumber, the market stall was paltry today, squash
bruised to touch, the fingerling potatoes muddy.

I like them with pepper, a crumbling of baguette.
We light taper candles to give the meal

a crown. The *sangria* you made with ice
and lemon and real cane sugar. I fish out morsels of

cherry and apple with bare fingers.
What we do not say crowds us with manic teeth:

the failing light, the junkyard coffins,
the forests receiving bodies like a wife.

The names, they shutter with distant lights:
Gaza. Homs. Alexandria. O, Damascus.

II

Anne

Winter trees are comrades in tragedy, each lit street
birthing shadows to walk through.

Even Jericho had me reading your orphan poems.
The sky's throat—

everycolor blue and a watercolor heart.
Lonely I unloved the cliffs, unpeeled a dress.

The sheets smelt of semen and lavender. What romance
did you hunt for in Bostonian pubs,

your orchid of little deaths?
Your thin white arms encircle themselves.

I can show you a city torching itself.
The sea eats the sea like firewood.

Coveting cheapens and, alone, we are stone sharks
gurgling water in a fountain.

I never mistook bread for kissing.
Anne, did you love your lover walking away?

You are edible, dear,
As hopelessly female as the moon.

Of the MRI Images for My Abdomen

A swamp of white.

So the secret is I glow.

      Blush with dust and ephemeral lungs.

This is my architecture, mineral
        and air, what I have always suspected:
            I am clamorous. I am a

paper daughter.

Theater vessel, ovaries charming as nests.
Wraithlike
      masonry, grainy as sugar.

Disrobe me and I am a cotillion dress, bone white
crocus
        and hungry as a milkweed.

I am a fence of lamplike
bones.

I would like another name now, in Gaelic
        or Sanskrit,
      meaning *hushed* or

the grain after fire.

I have earned it: the only edifice I own
                and what astonishing
gratitude

to know that beneath and below and
             beyond—

think of sand covered briefly,
shockingly,
        by snow—

there is something cluttered, and beautiful.

On My Shoulder a Bruise Yellows

In the end it is the timid that stays:
        some rare bird
outside a Midwestern motel room

or the faint wing of the *aleph*
        on an inscribed scroll of Quran.

I knew a photographer who scratched
his camera lens with
        scraps of tinfoil for bizarre light.

Half a decade since predawn
dappled brutal,
        redglow dusting the levee tents.

Either you left or his lungs flowered crisp
        again, grotto of breath. Atlas,

I curate the forgotten, stretch clotheslines
tight to
        pin mementos:

the lightning, the city trees
        erupting with petals,
even the golden hair buried in sand.

And the only dream where he lifts his head
to ask,

     Where is the island?

In the darkroom I hoard.
     Squinting in the red light
for silhouettes to tumble across the paper.

O my squandered,
     some train in Vierzon
clattered me awake before I could say

near France, north of Venice,
     beneath a circlet of hills where the villagers

worship a tin Mary and in summers
     pomegranates grow from dark green shrubs,

lush and red and enormous.

After Thunderstorms in Oklahoma

The sky becomes sickly,
unripe mango rind dappled
with flecks of green. Air opens
and closes like trachea. This
was the sky I dreamt in Ramallah,
a false awakening in the hotel room.
I pulled at curtains against the
whistling storm. But the curtains
swarmed into wood splintering my
fingers. I spun the wood into glass
and played it like a sitar. Outside
the sky roared and a forest sprouted,
abruptly, on the tiny bed. I crept
into the spruces and lay flat
on the rug. Cicadas rustled
inside a pear. The storm became
a militia. They jangled with chimes,
coming for my teeth. I woke
and it was sun and I forgot.

How to be a Duck in Paris

July, La Seine

make a palace of the bridge
        arcing

with silver

and count your   daughters

it is clean alchemy and only with eyes
stagnant—

fit for a
       stuffing—

will you trick the lumbering bodies

suspended above
legs   dangling with ordinary

magic

they speak of the coming decade
and their average

      wrecked hearts

when the cry snares
glassing   your throat

scatter it across the sky the water
          is jade

with the perished

Laleh

The night of the knives
Jupiter slung low
and silver in the sky.
A second moon,
the aunts said, rolling
rice into spheres.
The fighting crackled
outside our window
with the legs of a
hurricane. The aunts cut
lemons from Tabriz
for juice. The men
returned ruined and
we scoured the blood
from their shirts and
kissed them asleep.
That was lunging—
the welting of skin and
pockmarking, the reeds
glistening in river water,
a seashell stolen from
the Gulf on the mantle,
pearly, beautiful,
reminding us of what
we could not touch.

Origin

I.
I always imagine Zelda
      as a yawning figure,

emerging into daylight

      with a squiggle of blue ink
on her cheek.

Maybe she cracks the ice
with her teeth, the way the Aztecs

did with bones when it was time
for maize.   She drinks

straight from the faucet.

II.
Yesterday I found out that
Gaza

means *treasure*. I wanted to take this
astonishing fact to anyone

     but it was 4 am
on a Monday

and so I just clicked through the
internet photographs

      of children threading arms

through massive
surf,

a burnt shore.
One photograph showed a fish

      poisoned by phosphorus,
foaming at the gills.

The Gazania flower grows in
lemons and reds in Africa.

      The petal is rough as tongue.

Lizard

Before the clouds marshaled there were men
clamping rumpled maps in their fists.
Gunpowder lit the birch island
and a little village arose
amongst the dusty citrus groves and bees.

We sleep here now,
the wounded bricks rising
like mortar from the river. In the morning,

      a paper roof collapses over the warm
nectarines we keep sheltered from the ants.

No cocktail hour on this island, only the twin torchlights
of us, naked and showered and clothed again. If it rains,
we eat the noodles still crunchy from the package
and sing Kurt Cobain back into breathing
another trembled verse. Misfortune is an atlas
in British hands, cut, quartered, and each crossing asks

      fury or love? I wake
like an arabesque, to the scuffle of tiny legs

outside the window. The first pilgrims
gasped at the stretch of gold and
green. History apes that moment,
over and over, of delight at finding the already

found, and in my palm a tail
twitches like a miniature dinosaur. You,

my Telemachus,
abdomen bared, beard dirty—

I love you like a quickening,
like the last few steps home, dashing,
to show you what I've caught.

Legacy, As Explained by a Parisian Sculptress in a Bar

It is like flocking bones
for a   funeral.

Some winterish panorama
and a ghost rose waning in a cage
with ivory tines.

A long strip of skyscrapers tremor
on Sixth

Avenue and on the twenty-third floor
a finger presses a button and
machines thrum   alive,

a screen blinks photographs of dead Syrians
and a Cherokee legend
about buffalos.

                    No,

not the salivating grandmother marching
onion white
hands along some   eyelet
duvet for a red-hooded girl,

not Eve &
the sister in her legs. The exact *second*

fire licks the sand house into crystal in the

birthday   dream
and you realize you will   die inside

this glass hell
and instead of running or   sobbing,

you scuttle around like a maniac

touching the glass chimney and glass
pillow
          and even the   ice
rattling the glass bathtub.

You leave as many
fingerprints   as you can.

For Flinching

It may be a sputtered lightbulb or lost footing
one morning, a squinting and you will see it—
the dead wasp of your malice,
that *buzz hum buzz* milk still beading the stinger and
dust filming each eye. You will see it, arithmetic of *after*.
Septic. The wound you gifted. Little
composer, it was a wedding cake, that winter,
limp with earthquake and the crash of lobbed doors.
I release you to yourself. Some adobe hut trimmed with cacti,
or a skyscraper in Los Angeles. And, everywhere,
reminders like milk teeth: the insect detritus. Tiny limbs
on your carpet. A crinkled wing, radiant in your meat.

Al Aqsa

The line is full of irritated tourists.
We are late,
the clock has chimed and a man
sitting at the entrance is turning
people away.
A woman bemoans the wasted hour, shaking
her light hair loose beneath a scarf.
I stumble shy
as a lover and the man
lifts an eyebrow.

Muslim?

Yes,
I begged Allah in the quiet dark
of grass as a girl, trailed sand on paper and whispered
for lamplight.
The man asks me to recite the Fatiha and I say
the words—old, familiar
as bread—
with shoulders flat against the sunned stones.

Please, sister, your wrists.

How to say—
yes, under Detroit and Istanbul suns
love rafters me when the *muezzin* begins that slow
luxuriant rumble. I tug my sleeves lower.

Beneath bare feet the mosque carpet
rasps. Calligraphy flowers.

Here the Prophet drank milk.

In the courtyard the pillars scorch
and my father's accent
tides everywhere.

Hips

Heat comes from Saudi in billows,

the bar smoke and candles
as women

hold ice cubes to their temples.
I say *yalla* and he murmurs

the hills rolling sea
green through east Ireland.

The vermilion of flowers unfurled

his sleep the night
bombs exploded near the base

where he kept his uniform and cigarettes,
cheap menthols.

A mile from the holy Dome

and he longs for the
salt of his mother's broth, the sable-

armed tree that clears cobwebs
from the sky.

I hear him call land
daughter and, like a damsel,

I'm halved.

For two nights I dream of him
appearing on a bridge,

lifting me by the hip. Done over,
I would lean in.

I would give myself like fossil.

The Immigrant's Children

A firework sizzles above
our heads. We pray. *Allah,*
Allah. The graveyard shines
with rain. Unlaced, we are
the daughters with overfed
beds, a warrior's faith. Blue
dollops on the canvas as we
mural dancing trees, two
jade birds. The dead cry out
from the harbor, doleful.
In our sleep, we are islands.
Each limb is a flag.

Even Fevers Make Bodies

Jerusalem springs forth like a violence
and I
       audacious sashay

her gulfing streets with twin wings on my shoulder.

     Mouth,
I have skin soft enough to catch you

and the pink below the needle—
rot, rot.

Pinned beneath opium eyes I pitched
myself across

     the Atlantic. Celtic music kept pace of our lungs.

Root, you microscopic, sly thing.

Even teethed by a lover my organs pulse for certain cities.

I saw a woman on a porch once. Her hair, silver as tusks,
     swung

polished in the simple Vienna light.

She said comets spin on these July
evenings

because Allah loves to dance in their
lovely glow.

Happy

I love the dusks of Abu
Dhabi, sky dappled like
fig flesh, that gentle
dying light. Wavering.
The magic of coals. My
body when you light it
like an orchard. The one
who filled a suitcase
with river and danced.
A word in Barcelona,
muffled soft as cashmere,
while rain falls and the
birds begin to wake.

Attic's Window

The wooden room is orphaned,
lonely as Penelope, and dragonflies drum hopeful
against the glass. In a photograph, a tree stands ashen,
bark as bone in the faint winter light. Her arms are empty,
and this is your mother's heirloom. Tuesday,
the sky is orange, rippling with birds. A child drew this,
all of it: house, storm, insect, a stick figure mourning
over a goldfish, crying big cerulean tears. Even the scraggly
shoreline, the hills flung with citadels. On the bus a man
sings Oum Kalthoum and I am thinking of New Zealand,
of how the water must be cold on his shoulders now,
and how love can be a punishment for the gluttony
of wanting. Of wanting, when a loamy eyed little girl
climbs onto my lap and taps at the landscape
smudging outside the bus. Of wanting, when she cries
because her biscuit is finished, and then sleeps, heavy
in my arms, crumbs clinging to her mouth. At Nablus,
the mother shepherds her other children off the bus,
laughing. She apologizes for the little girl and I am still
caught in the dizzying sun of Auckland, without language as
I lift the girl still sticky with tears and return her
and her humid scent of grass.

Fruit

You of the moist
eyes and rough mouth.
I glitter like dew for
your gaze and write
Morocco in dust
with fingertips. Sun
finds you flung
across an orchard of
music tapping along
with bare feet in rain
and grass. I never
weep and neither
should you: The birds
know nothing of greed
or the love we
splintered together
in urban streets.
Undressing makes
confetti of the night
and I am a slowly lit
Roman candle that all
the neighborhood
children—sleepy, tipsy
with August—have
gathered to watch burn.

Remember

For Reem Harb

Fingernails.

In the distance between each planet
is a story

of men and women arguing
holding onto things

too hot and precious and human to bear.

Like yours:
flames

shooting high as skyscrapers
from lunatic hands

or the poison that was being sprinkled
on your lentils.

You walked into a house where my father
was a little boy

wore thigh high boots and a knot of red scarf.

A house of Quran
my grandfather saw your legs

kicked you out

and no one has a photograph.

Did you find it small—
this life of ink on

satinet—

dewing the fabric but, also, ruining it?

Or did you love spoons for their kind stature,
the click

of hunger?

All before the shutters lowered like monsoon
season

before your brain flowered into an oil
spill

and you thought you were
Arafat's bride.

The most beautiful woman in the world.

Souvenirs

I.

Wind churning a daub of Haifa seawater into my eye. Tomorrow,
a strip of sunburn,

skin peeling auburn.

II.

Word scuffing my throat at Qalandiya checkpoint
as a man nods and

click rotates metal bars. Word rasps at Ramallah windows facing
always

the burly settlements—*No*—even during autumn

weddings. Word nests like a sunflower seed between
teeth and only

later do I spit it out

beneath a harvest moon in Manhattan.

III.

Hot cheek kiss from Jimmy. Naming the dead, and their
cities. Hawaii

ambered his eyes and Jerusalem keening

for Shabbat as we strode the dawn.

IV.

A photograph of the sunlit souk: prayer
beads,

      kaffiyehs, ceramics, carpet. Finger pricked on the crown

of thorns fashioned out of cedar wood.

V.

Shukran from the Palestinian shopkeeper when I translated
to the American women for him:

no the kitten is his not injured she likes to sleep in the tire

      Blond eyebrows knitted

and when they left, the shopkeeper shrugged and said— bemused,
wondering—

    The Americans, their hearts bleed for cats.

For Lent

S, I dreamt we draped fairy lights around the Coliseum,
roping the tangled wires into snakelike piers. God

whispered from a wasp nest. You ate the candy
skull. Later, it was water rising in scarlet waves,

a shark speaking your name. Firewood or lace or rifle,
I house the timid of you in my mouth, seven languages

before steeple. Our passports are soaked, and ruined.
Budapest glows and snowflakes frame the false memory:

we swam in an ocean of pollen, yellow so thick it trembled
against our bodies. You tapped the gold from my hair.

Marketplace

A quartet of chickens squawk
and the smell is cinnamon and
shit. One man calls out to me in
Hebrew, another Arabic. Both
carry crates. A peddler says his
necklace of gold and orange
beads will help me marry, and
some teenagers grin, flash teeth
coconut white as the *muezzin*
calls for prayer, for the pull of
bodies tired and brown and soft
to the ground, as though God
spread this land like a gypsy's
pillowcase, littered with silver
hills and slinging rivers, stars
like a scarab pendant. I ask for
Gaza, and a woman ushers a
piece of bread into my mouth,
says the art is in the pinchful
of sumac. The city—an engine,
a specimen—turns with the
voices peddling mixed candies,
almonds, veils the precise tint
of pomegranate flesh, tin stars
painted white. *Bateekh bateekh,
kousa kousa*. I smell like dirt,
or bread. A boy at the refugee
camp taps his cigarette, waves

widely as though he is erasing
something. Every day I walk the
winding road east to the cluster
of buses. I ask for Nablus. I ask
for Hebron. I ask for Jaffa.

Listen,

she says,
your hands might be cold but the sun will reach us

soon. Five decades ahead of me,

she finds certain accessories trifling: gloves, cigarettes,
hairbrush. Hamsa necklace

and a plate decorated with hieroglyphics,
this is tea.

An Egyptian suitor, she laughs, many years ago,

asked her to marry by the Red Sea.
And then a Moroccan, two Iraqis. Her with sepia hair

and a face like porcelain.

She sighs. It was ruin to be loved
like that, waking to desert

hyacinths
and lace gowns sewn by deft Parisian fingers.

Almonds crunch between our teeth as the *muezzin* begins.

From the ascent,
she points to the hill where a prophet knelt

to touch soil.

I ask about the lace, if it itched. No, she muses, but the
roses

always brought beetles and a rash.

When she finally wed,
it was a farmer's son, poor, but with kind eyes and hands

that always smelled of oranges.
Listen, she scolds,

enough of this heartbreak talk. Drink your tea.

In the winter she would boil
jasmine, dozens of petals at once, and dip her hair

slowly in the steam. Listen,
she says,

her eyes suddenly
serious, he might be dead but not loving anyone

else won't bring him back.

Her wedding night, she and the farmer's son made love
like bread,

her voice rising with her body.
This was Jaffa,

1946, and they kept the window open, for the air,
for the moon.

Assembling

At the water's border
you are cupping sand for crafted forests.

Evergreen, evergreen.

I sang to you about wings, seeds,
January. I skull your absence

with six months.

This is how the ocean rises,
lavender blue as it rains.

Sketch my lips on paper.
The open-

mouthed sigh when your brother
lit the paper lanterns

and we released them into the
Christmas sky.

We watched the colors,
then went inside to the burning wood.

Mount

At the top the hill dips clefted
over the granite. Coffins cluster
between the groves of green-
tipped olive shrubs. A man shovels
dirt, the blade copper in the sun.
He shuffles soil for a new grave,
intent on his task (tiny in this
monstrous land), ignoring the
Indian tourists rustling maps and
the Austrian men arguing about
soccer over flasks. Was it an olive
in the hands of a woman choking
dirty water in the camps (the other
camps, not the camps of Sabra
Baqa'a Zarqa Rashidieh Kalandia
Khan Yunis Jabalia Aida Shatila)?
Was it an olive steadied between the
teeth of one who spoke *god* and
lived another sun? Was the olive
the clay, then, was it the air that
kept bodies alive and hurtled
across the sea for this crescent
of land? The ancients said
plants took the scent of their
tenders. When they ate a leaf,
they thanked the hand that
plucked it. Who picked the olives
that crowded a bowl on that first

table in 1948 Yazur Umm al-Faraj
Kafr Sabt Qira Ibdis Kafra Danna
Kudna Nitaf Saffuriyya Hatta
Ayn Ghazal Sajad Dimra Aqir?
And what was the taste as
tongue rolled over the sphere
what was the memory lodged
like scar onto that green skin?
Did you taste it, do you still taste
it—the salt from the hands that
shuffled life from the dirt bitter
salty and sharp as any truth.

Loving the Remains

We are waiting with peppered
lips for the city to revive herself,
Andalusia blood, vagrant love,
a luck like air. Sea as blue as
a sultan's jewels, a sky white, rain's
blooming, rose carved from ivory.
No coffee grains scattering into
an immigrant's fortune, we wear
our cities like helmets. We are
thieves, filching a language
for its pearls, groves, farewell.

Akko, and the Sun Sets

For Salim Salem

There is something of the dreaming
in the coastline, a vapor to that
gold. Horizon blazes eccentric red,
a family of women and children
eating on the shore. There is something,
dreaming, this walking has blistered, sandal
tatters past the mosques, the stone courtyard,
the rugs flapping like tongues as one tosses
and another swings the tree branch, earth
scattering, charging the sunlight. That thwack,
thwack ricochets out like paean with the *oud*
unstrung. Nothing to eat but sugar:
Sha'ar al banat. Knafeh. Tangerine ice cream.
Sorbet numbs teeth, a drop on collarbone
and the skin sticky, burnt. Allah is crooned awake.
A man unrolls an ivory rug on the rockline, begins
to pray. Birds billow nameless, cry to one another, a
seagull dashes a white swoop. Daylight still, but the moon
steams with seven eyes. A pluming sea sprawls
against the pale sand, foam whirling red
as Indian ruby, or kidney. The man bends
on the rug and flecks of sea settle on him like little
snow. It is summer and the rocks are dusty
and my grandfather was born here.

Acknowledgments

Thank you to Angela Leroux-Lindsey, whose faith in this book brought it to life. I am grateful to Diane Goettel and Black Lawrence Press for being so lovely to work with. Thank you to Fady Joudah for his immeasurable support.

I am absurdly lucky to be surrounded by incredible family and friends: Talal, Johnny, Miriam, Hanine, Nafez, Omar, Layal. You inspire me.

Hala Alyan is a Palestinian American poet and clinical psychologist whose work has appeared in numerous journals including *The Missouri Review*, *Prairie Schooner* and *Colorado Review*. Her first full-length poetry collection, *ATRIUM* (Three Rooms Press), was awarded the 2013 Arab American Book Award in Poetry. Her collection *HIJRA* was selected as a winner of the 2015 Crab Orchard Series in Poetry and will be published by Southern Illinois University Press. She resides in Manhattan.